From Your Friends At **The MAILBOX®**

MAY

A MONTH OF REPRODUCIBLES AT YOUR FINGERTIPS!

Kindergarten

Editor:
Angie Kutzer

Contributing Editor:
Mackie Rhodes

Writers:
Joe Appleton, Susan Bunyan, Marilee Burton, Rhonda Dominguez,
Diane Gilliam, Lucia Kemp Henry, Kathleen Padilla, Kelli Plaxco

Art Coordinator:
Clevell Harris

Artists:
Cathy Spangler Bruce, Susan Bunyan,
Clevell Harris, Lucia Kemp Henry,
Kimberly Richard, Rebecca Saunders,
Barry Slate, Donna K. Teal

Cover Artist:
Jennifer Tipton Bennett

www.themailbox.com

©1998 by THE EDUCATION CENTER, INC.
All rights reserved.
ISBN10 #1-56234-229-0 • ISBN13 # 978-156234-229-6

Manufactured in the United States
10 9 8 7 6 5 4

Table Of Contents

MEETINGS:

To Do:

Special Dates:

MAY
Classroom Themes:

Books To Check Out:

Materials To Collect:

Duties This Month:

Birthdays:

MAY

Be Kind To ANIMALS WEEK ®

Here's a "pet-pourri" of ideas to use during this weeklong observation held annually during the first full week of May. The event, sponsored by the American Humane Association, promotes kindness to and humane care of animals.

First, The Legwork...

Youngsters will get a leg up on some counting and classifying skills with this activity. To begin, have students brainstorm as many different pets as possible. List their responses on chart paper. Discuss with youngsters ways in which each named pet can be cared for. Then have volunteers label each animal name with a colored sticky dot that corresponds to its number of legs. For example, two-legged pets might be labeled with blue dots, whereas four-legged pets are marked with red dots. Count the dots in each color; then compare the results. Are any of the listed pets no-legged animals? Reproduce page 6 as a follow-up activity for independent practice.

They Come In All Sizes

Help students size up the responsibilities of pet ownership with this idea. Refer students back to the list of pets in "First, The Legwork…"; then have them compare the sizes of animals with the same number of legs. Are all the two-legged animals the same size? The four-legged animals? After establishing that the animals in each leg category vary in size, lead students in a discussion about how housing and caring for a larger pet might differ from that of a smaller pet. For example, a horse needs plenty of outdoor space, a large shelter, and lots of food. In comparison, a hamster can be housed and exercised in a small cage and needs relatively little food. Give each child a copy of page 7. Have her color and cut out the animal pictures, then glue them in the boxes from smallest to largest.

Creature Kindnesses

Give youngsters the opportunity to practice a little kindness with these personalized pet creations. For each child, duplicate a construction-paper copy of the animal pattern on page 8. To make a pet, cut out the animal body and head; then fold the body cutout and cut the slit as indicated. Use craft items to decorate the body and head to represent a four-legged pet of your choosing. Then stand the body on a table and insert the head into the slit. If appropriate, add a tail made from a craft item, such as a pipe cleaner, a pom-pom, or yarn. (If desired, decorate additional enlarged or reduced copies of the pattern to create an entire pet family.) Then invite each child to take her special creature(s) to the dramatic-play area to practice some kind and conscientious caretaking.

We've Got Legs!

Count.
Write.
Color.

How many animals have **0** legs? ☐

How many animals have **2** legs? ☐

How many animals have **4** legs? ☐

How many animals have **8** legs? ☐

Bonus Box: How many animal legs are in the picture?

Name_____

They Come In All Sizes

Color.

Cut.

Sequence by size.

Glue.

Animal Pattern
Use with "Creature Kindnesses" on page 5.

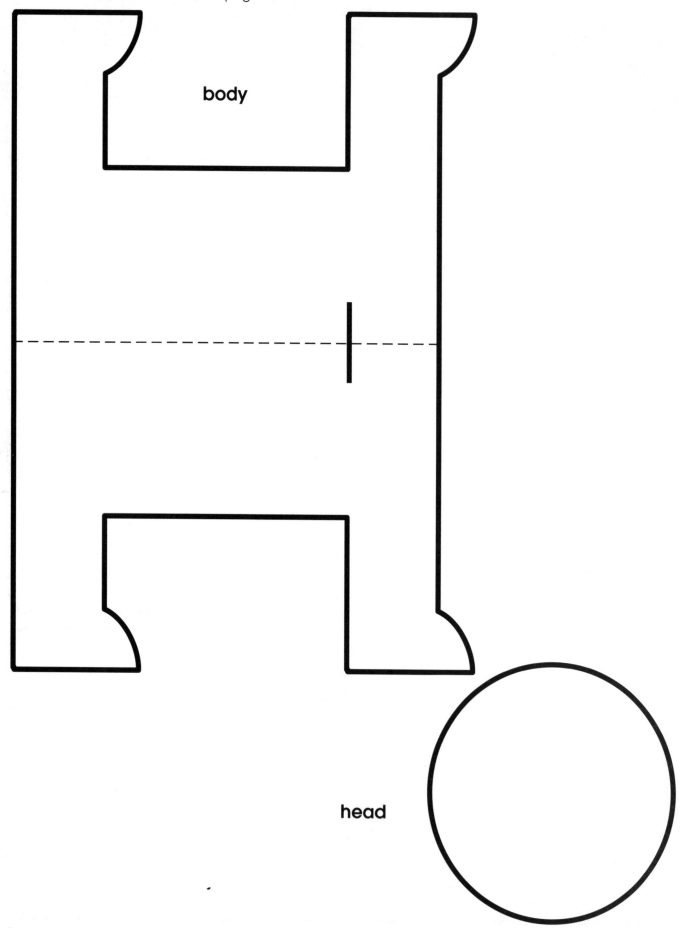

body

head

Blooms And Blossoms

Growing minds will blossom with these fresh floral ideas. It's flower power!

Flower Walk

Pick a nice sunny day to pull up roots and take this flower-filled tour to observe your school's blooms and blossoms. For the tour, equip each child with a copy of the observation sheet on page 11, a clipboard, and crayons or markers. Then take a leisurely walk around the school grounds to look for flowers of all colors. Have each youngster draw the different flowers observed onto his observation form. Back in the classroom, invite him to share his illustrations with the class. Then graph students' flower finds by color to discover which flower color is most common around your school.

Name ___Joey___
Flower Walk
Draw the flowers you see.

A Floral Spell

Cast a spell on youngsters with this fragrant version of the popular game Hangman. To prepare, duplicate the game pieces on page 12 onto white construction paper. Color, cut out, and laminate each game piece; then attach magnetic tape to the back of each piece. To play, choose a student's name, a sight word, or another familiar word from the classroom. Draw a line for each letter of the word on a magnetic chalkboard. Have each player guess a letter. If the letter is in the word, write it on the appropriate line. If it is not in the word, write the letter at the bottom of the board; then place a flower piece on the board. Encourage your youngsters to guess the letters and name the word correctly before all the pieces are used to assemble the flower.

Petal Patterns

Inject some flower power into youngsters' patterning knowledge with these tell-all petal patterns. To prepare the manipulatives, duplicate and cut out a supply of colored construction-paper flowers using the patterns on page 13. Glue some of the flower cutouts onto separate sentence strips to create ABAB, AABAAB, ABBABB, AABBAABB, and ABCABC patterns. Program the back of each pattern strip with the pattern type represented on the front; then program a separate note card with each pattern type. Explain to students how each pattern type is determined. Then invite volunteers to match each card to its corresponding flower pattern. Have them check the back of each pattern strip for correctness; then instruct youngsters to extend the pattern on each strip with the leftover flower cutouts. If desired, place the pattern strips, cards, and flower cutouts in a center to encourage continued practice. For individual assessment, give each child a copy of page 14 to complete.

ABAB

Bingo Blossoms

Youngsters' word-recognition skills will come into full bloom with this flowery bingo game. Duplicate a class set of construction-paper bingo cards (page 15). Program each flower petal on each card with a sight word, making sure each card is different; then cut out and laminate the cards. To create caller cards, label a separate notecard with each sight word represented on the bingo cards. Establish with students the guidelines for completing a card. For example, a card might be complete after all the petals are covered, or perhaps three side by side might be the agreed-upon criteria. Appoint a caller, give each child a bingo card and a supply of sunflower-seed counters, and then watch the fun blossom!

Bingo Blossoms

will · I · you · can · not · me

Bingo Blossoms

by · it · can · will · we · is

Odd Or Even?

Bouquets of blossoms are the perfect seasonal pick to teach students about odd and even sets. To prepare, duplicate and cut out 55 construction-paper flowers using the patterns on page 13. Place one to ten cutouts into each of ten zippered plastic bags. (You might prepare additional bags so that one bag is available for every two children.) Group students into pairs; then invite each pair to select a bagged bouquet of flowers. Ask the partners to distribute the flowers evenly between themselves so that each receives her "fair" share. When youngsters discover that not all the blossom sets can be distributed evenly—that the uneven distributions are "not fair"—explain that those bags contain an odd number of flowers. Write the odd numerals under the heading "Odd" on the chalkboard. Tell youngsters that the other bags contain an even number of flowers. Write those numerals under "Even." Then give each child a copy of page 16 to complete. Review the page with your youngsters so that they can compare their results.

Odd
3
7

Even
2
6
4

Flower Power

Just how much power is in a flower? Discover the answer with this incentive idea. Show youngsters a set of large, laminated, die-cut letters that spell "flower." Explain that you will display a letter each time students are caught randomly engaging in a specified desirable behavior, such as helping a classmate or using courtesy words. Throughout the day, when youngsters are spontaneously exhibiting the targeted behavior(s), surprise them by posting a letter. After the word is completely spelled out, reward students with a special privilege, such as extra free choice time or a round of a favorite game. As an alternative to spelling the word, use the game pieces made in "A Floral Spell" on page 9. After the flower is assembled, offer the class a special privilege.

Name _____

Flower Walk

Draw the flowers you see.

11

petals

flower center

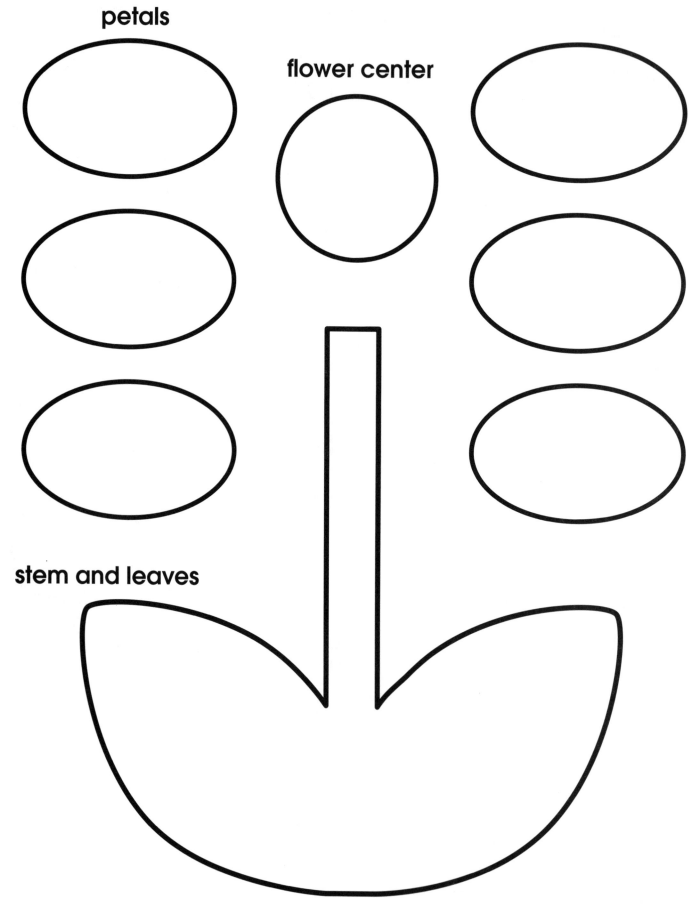

stem and leaves

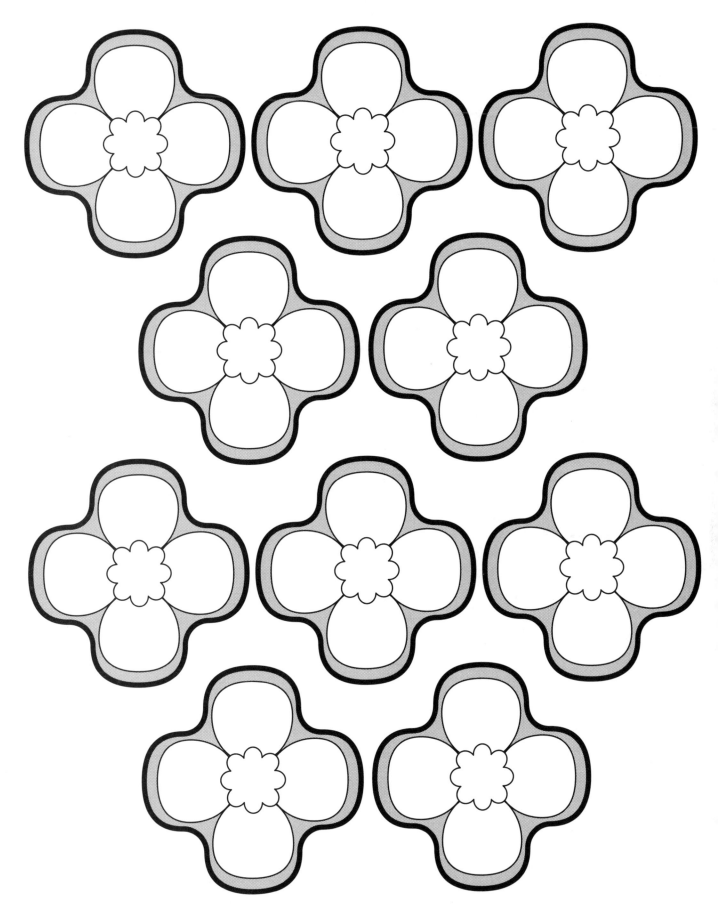

Name _____

Petal Patterns

Label each pattern.

Bonus Box: Draw a flower pattern on the back of your paper. Ask a friend to name the pattern type.

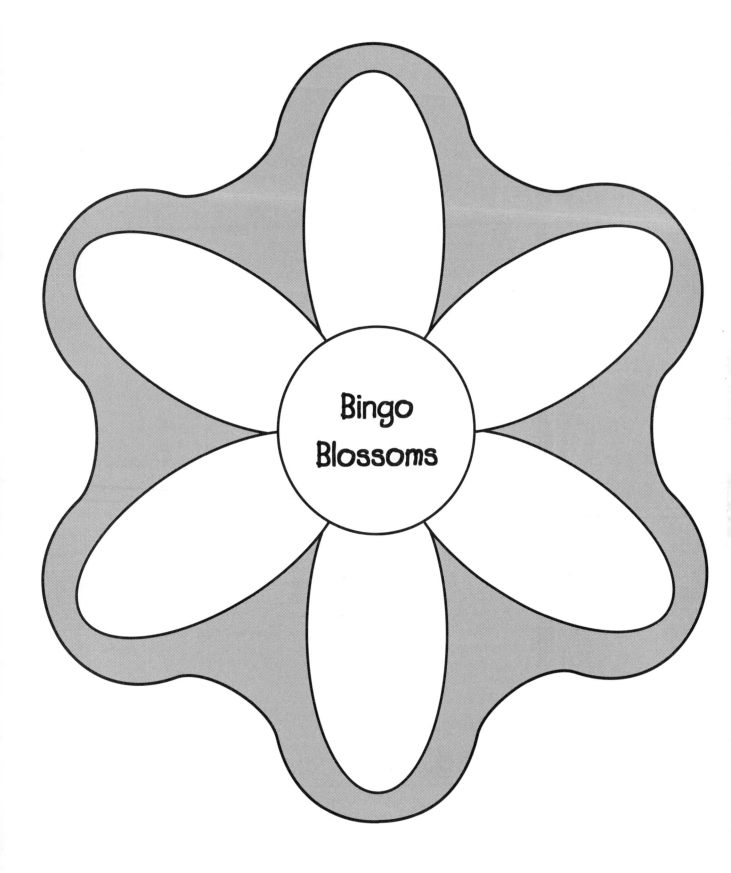

Bingo
Blossoms

Name _____

Odd Or Even?

Count the flowers.

Write the numeral.

Fill in the boxes.

The **odd** numerals are:

The **even** numerals are:

Marvelous MOMS & Dandy DADS

Mother's Day and Father's Day are the perfect times to pay tribute to well-deserving parents and primary caregivers—but these activities are so much fun that youngsters will love doing them anytime!

Happy Mothe

My mom makes me smile when my mom makes me ___pancakes___ .

Mom Makes Me Smile

Imagine the many mommy-smiles when your little ones deliver these yummy tributes to their moms. To prepare, program a sheet of paper with "My mom makes me smile when my mom makes me _____." Then duplicate a class supply of the page. Lead your students in a discussion about favorite foods that their mothers prepare. Write each child's favorite mommy-made food on her paper; then have her illustrate the page. Glue each illustration onto a sheet of construction paper. After the glue dries, fold the paper in half greeting-card style. Have each child illustrate her card cover with her own smiling self-portrait; then write any dictated message on her card.

What A Day Dad Had!

Dad's had quite a day! And so will youngsters when they create these special daddy books that strengthen word-family skills. Duplicate a class quantity plus two copies of the booklet pages on page 18 onto construction paper. Color and cut apart the two extra copies. Staple one set of pages between tagboard covers. Title the booklet "Dad's Day." Then trim each sentence off the bottom of each page in the second set of pages. Glue each picture onto a sentence strip; then copy the corresponding sentence on the strip.

To use, read the sample booklet to the class. Then use the sentence strips to point out the -ad family words and the predictable sentence patterns. Afterward, invite each youngster to make a "Dad's Day" booklet to read to his own dad.

A Crowning Occasion

These "hand-some" crowns are the perfect way to top off parents' special days. To make one, have a child hold her fingers and thumb close together as you trace her hand several times onto construction paper. Ask her to cut out each hand outline; then have the child glue the cutouts onto a tagboard headband. Invite her to decorate the resulting crown with glitter-paint or gold craft-paint fingerprints. Then adjust the crown to fit an average adult's head, and staple the ends together. Encourage each child to crown her mom and dad on their respective special days—as part of the royal treatment planned for each of them!

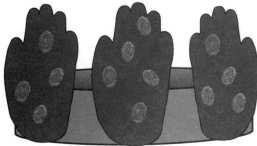

Color. Cut. Staple. Read.

Dad had a bad day. 1

Dad had a mad day. 2

Dad had a sad day. 3

Dad had a glad day. 4

Dad had a Dad's day! 5

Dad	mad
had	sad
bad	glad

6

NATIONAL PHYSICAL FITNESS AND SPORTS MONTH

Get youngsters' health in good shape this month with a salute to physical fitness. These fitting activities are sure to give each child's mind *and* body a healthful workout!

Time To Take Action

Set students' minds in motion with this mental exercise. Ask them to brainstorm a list of physical activities that are healthful and easily accessible, from team sports to yard work to solo recreational activities. Write their responses on chart paper; then highlight and discuss the activities that each child can do at home, in school, or in his neighborhood. Send home a list of activities with each child to encourage physical fitness at home as well as at school. Extend your brainstorming session by challenging youngsters to take action. To practice the action-taking step, divide your class into small groups. Assign each group a highlighted activity; then have the group mime or perform (if appropriate) the activity. Afterward encourage youngsters to make some of these practices a daily habit. Practice makes perfectly good sense when it comes to healthful habits.

Fitness Pledge Posters

After their mental workouts and practice sessions, youngsters will be ready to make a pledge to keep their bodies physically fit. Duplicate the poster on page 20 for each child; then cut it out along the bold lines. Also cut out the circle as indicated on each copy. Review with the class the three key elements to physical fitness: *healthful eating habits, plenty of sleep,* and *exercise.* Then invite each child to make a fitness pledge poster.

To begin, ask each child to glue a few small magazine cutouts of healthful snacks onto her poster page. Help her determine a healthful bedtime; then write that time on the corresponding line. Write the child's dictated exercise choices on the appropriate lines. Then tape a copy of her photo to the back of her page so that her face shows through the opening. Have the child color the sports clothing with her favorite colors. Glue the poster onto construction paper; then have her create a sports-sticker or stamp border around the poster. Youngsters will feel like winners when they take their posters home to share with their families!

For Additional Information...

If you're interested in obtaining more information about National Physical Fitness And Sports Month, here's the agency to contact:

President's Council On Physical Fitness And Sports
HHH Building
200 Independence Ave., SW
Room 738H
Washington, DC 20201-0004
(202) 690-9000

My Fitness Pledge

I will eat **healthful** snacks.

Cut
this
out.

I will get plenty of **sleep.**

I will go to bed at _____.

I will gets lots of **exercise.** I will

1. _____

2. _____

3. _____

Westward, Ho!

If your "younguns" are wild about the West, here's a herd of ideas that is sure to lasso little learners' attention. Let's go! Westward, ho!

Round 'em Up

Rustle up some Wild West fun with this cow-corralling idea. To prepare, enlarge the cow pattern on page 26. Duplicate a class supply of this pattern onto construction paper; then laminate and cut out each pattern. Hide the cutouts around your classroom. Enlist students' help in creating a block corral in the art center; then have each of your little cowpokes round up a hidden cow and place it in the corral. During center time, invite each art center visitor to decorate a cow cutout with an assortment of craft supplies. After this rollicking roundup, youngsters are sure to be in the "moo-d" for more westward adventures.

Cactus Cuisine

Yee-ha! Here comes the chuck wagon—just in time for your little rustlers to whip up this tasty cactus cuisine. In advance, gather a class quantity of the items listed in the recipe on page 24. Duplicate and color an enlarged copy of the recipe; then display it in your cooking center. Invite each visitor to the center to create his own cactus snack following the directions in the recipe.

Since you've pricked their interest, why not extend this activity into a sequencing treat for youngsters? Simply duplicate the recipe for each child. Have him color and cut apart the directions; then direct him to glue the strips in sequence on construction paper. Encourage him to take his recipe home to share with his family. Delicious!

Cowpoke Concentration

Create some cowpoke memories with this Western-style Memory game. To prepare, duplicate and cut out two tagboard copies of the picture-card set on page 23. Color each matching pair identically; then laminate the cards for durability. Store the cards in a labeled, zippered plastic bag. To use them, randomly place the cards facedown. Have a player turn over two cards. If the cards match, she keeps them. If the cards do not match, the player returns them facedown to the playing surface. Have the players continue taking turns in this manner until all the matches are found.

Dandy Duds

Use these dandy duds to introduce youngsters to the fine art of Western wear. To begin, make tagboard tracers of the cowpoke patterns on pages 25 and 26. Supply your art center with the tracers and an assortment of craft items and materials—such as construction paper, gift wrap, wallpaper, and fabric. Invite each youngster to trace each of the clothing and accessory items on the material of her choice. Then instruct her to cut out the pieces. Also have her trace and cut out a construction-paper head. Direct the child to assemble the pieces on construction paper to create a cowpoke. Then invite her to use craft items to create the facial features and hair on her cowpoke. Display the students' creations with the title "Dandy Duds."

BETH

Buckaroo's Beans

This little buckaroo really counts on his beans! And so will your students with this counting activity. To make a buckaroo, enlarge and duplicate the cowpoke patterns (pages 25 and 26) onto construction paper. Also make additional copies of the hat pattern. Then assemble and glue all the pieces *except* the hats onto a sheet of tagboard. Add the facial features and hair using craft items; then program each hat with a different numeral. Place the buckaroo, hats, and a supply of dried beans in your math center. Explain that the numeral on each hat represents the number of beans the buckaroo ate for dinner. To use the activity, a student places a hat on the buckaroo's head. His partner counts out the corresponding number of beans onto the buckaroo's shirt. Then the partners count the beans together to check for accuracy. After each round, have the partners switch roles and continue play.

Rootin'-Tootin' Reading And Writing

Round up your little rustlers for this reading and writing rodeo. To create word cards, make a construction-paper copy of the picture cards on page 23. Color and cut out each card; then glue each onto a separate notecard. To make the cards self-checking, label the back of each card with the word for the picture. Then label another blank notecard with each picture's word. Laminate all the cards for durability.

To use them, put the word cards in a cowboy hat; then spread the picture cards faceup on a table. Have a child draw a card from the hat, find the corresponding picture card, and check his work. After students succeed at "reading" the word cards, place the card pairs in your writing center. Then invite students to use these words in their Wild West writing activities.

Use with "Cowpoke Concentration" on page 21 and "Rootin'-Tootin' Reading And Writing" on page 22.

Cactus Cuisine

You will need:

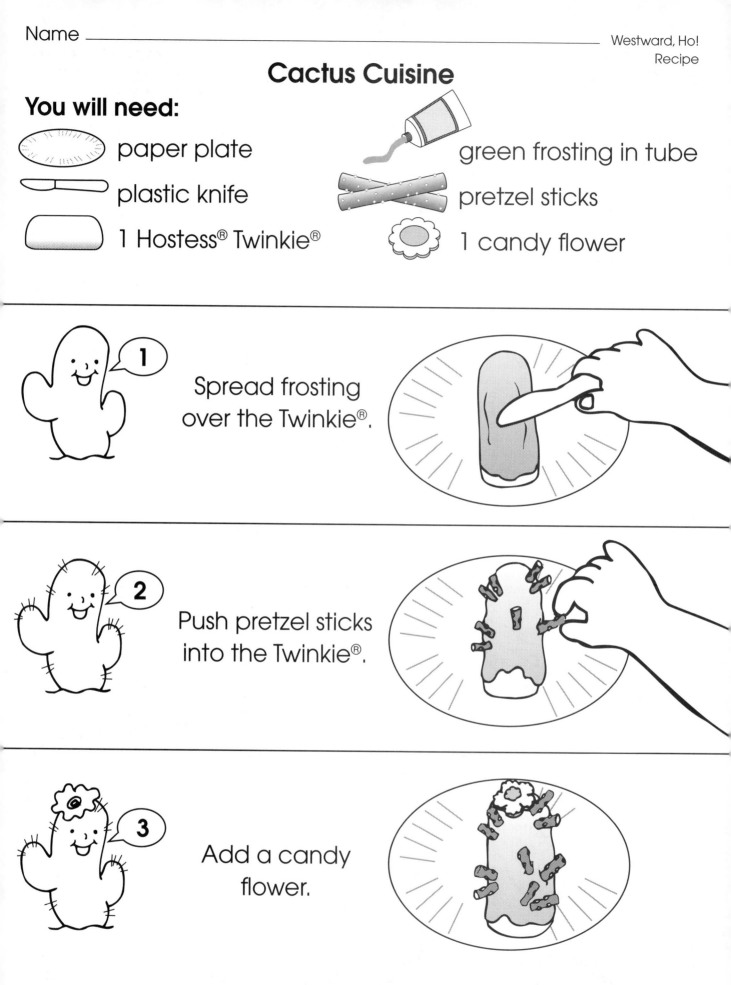

paper plate

plastic knife

1 Hostess® Twinkie®

green frosting in tube

pretzel sticks

1 candy flower

1 Spread frosting over the Twinkie®.

2 Push pretzel sticks into the Twinkie®.

3 Add a candy flower.

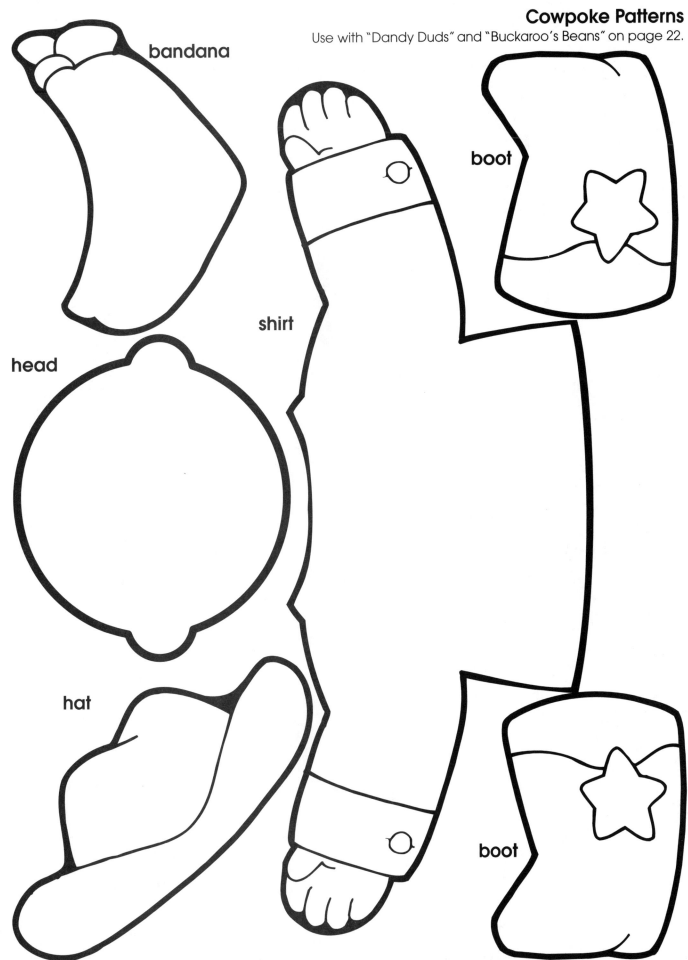

bandana

Cowpoke Patterns
Use with "Dandy Duds" and "Buckaroo's Beans" on page 22.

boot

shirt

head

hat

boot

Cowpoke Pattern
Use with "Dandy Duds" and "Buckaroo's Beans" on page 22.

chaps

Cow Pattern
Use with "Round 'em Up" on page 21.

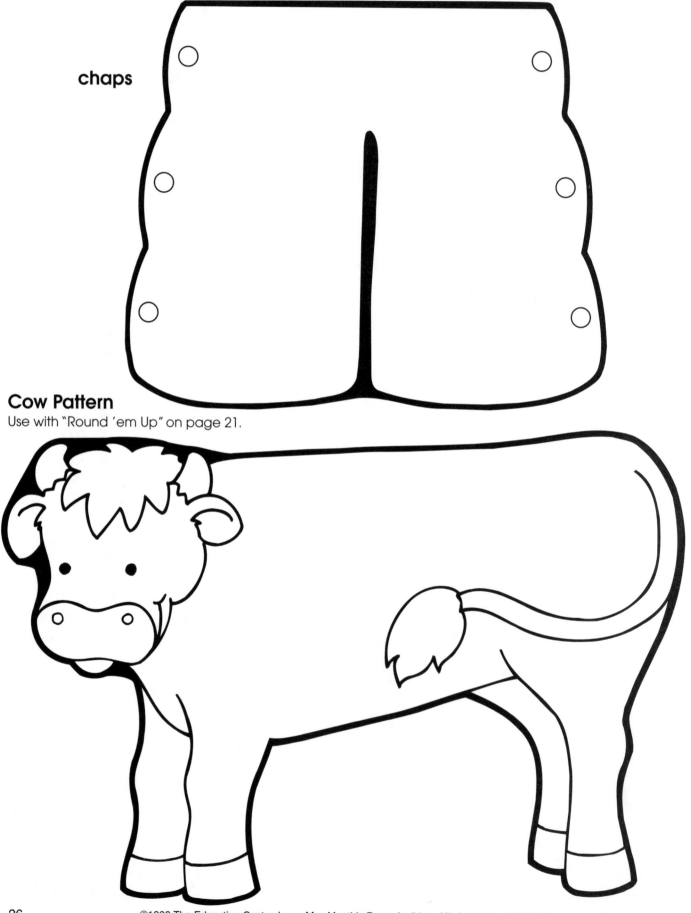

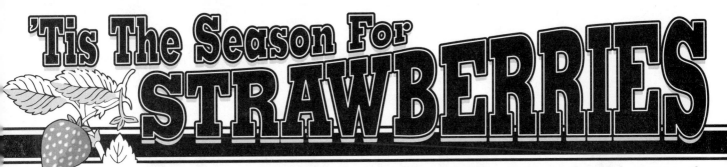

'Tis The Season For STRAWBERRIES

Conditions are "ripe" for these seasonal strawberry ideas. So pick some of these juicy activities to put youngsters in the mood for sunny days ahead!

Strawberry Toppings

Top off your strawberry storytime with these "berry" interesting hats. To begin, duplicate the hat pattern on page 28; then enlarge the pattern to 125 percent. Duplicate a class quantity of the enlarged pattern onto red construction paper (you may have to trim the construction paper to fit your copier), and cut each pattern out. Help each child trace her hand onto green construction paper; then have her cut out the resulting outline. To make a hat, cut the slits and punch holes in the strawberry cutout as indicated. Glue white hole-punch dots on the cutout to represent strawberry seeds. Overlap and glue the Xs over the Os at the top of the strawberry cutout. Curl the fingers of the hand cutout around a pencil; then glue the palm of the hand over the Xs to create the strawberry cap. Lace a length of yarn through the holes; then fit the hat to the child's head, tying the yarn ends into a bow under her chin. Invite youngsters to wear their special toppings and munch a few fresh strawberries while you read a strawberry story, such as *The Little Mouse, The Red Ripe Strawberry, And The Big Hungry Bear* by Don and Audrey Wood (Child's Play [International] Ltd) or Molly Bang's *The Grey Lady And The Strawberry Snatcher* (Aladdin Paperbacks).

Red Fruity Rolls

Youngsters will roll into some simple addition fun when they assume the roles of strawberry game pieces in this math game. Duplicate and cut out two tagboard die patterns (page 29). Color each die; then fold and glue each die as indicated. Tape a large circle on the floor to represent a bowl. Then invite students to don their strawberry hats (from "Strawberry Toppings") and cluster close together to resemble strawberries in a patch. Appoint two children to be strawberry pickers. To play, have each picker roll a die and then "pick" that number of strawberries from the patch to put in the bowl. Ask the class to count the sum of the two pickers' berries. Have the berries and pickers return to the patch; then appoint two different pickers. Continue the game until each child has played the role of a picker.

To Market, To Market

Send youngsters to the market to buy some fat strawberries—and to show off their spending savvy! Give each child a copy of page 30. Point out the price of strawberries at the market; then instruct him to cut out the coins and price tags at the bottom of the page. Have him glue each tag and coin in the appropriate box on his paper. Then invite him to color the picture. Reward each student's thrifty money skills with a few juicy strawberries to eat. Yum!

Hat Pattern

Use with "Strawberry Toppings" on page 27.

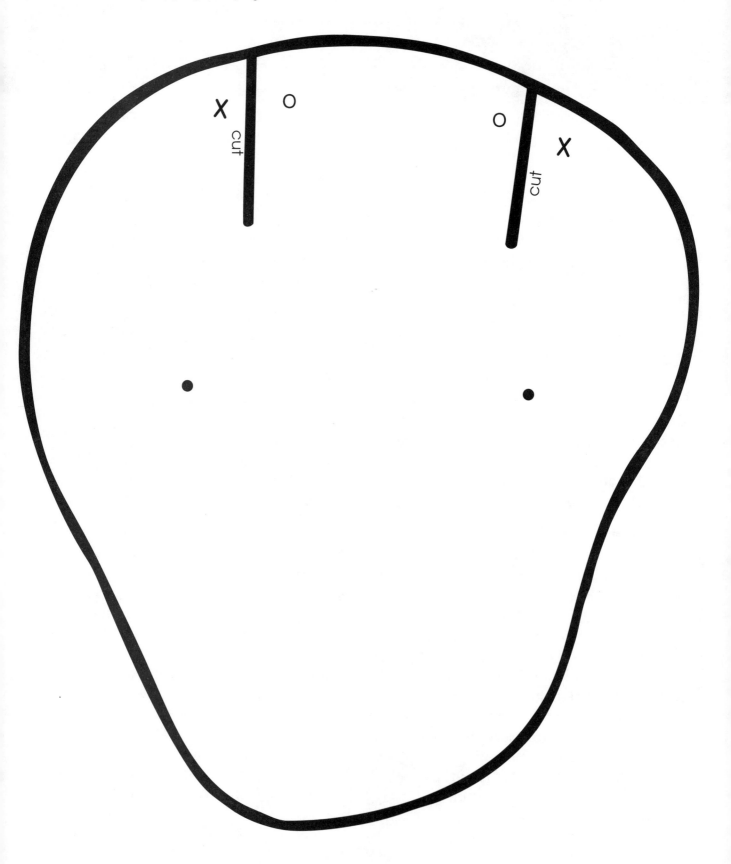

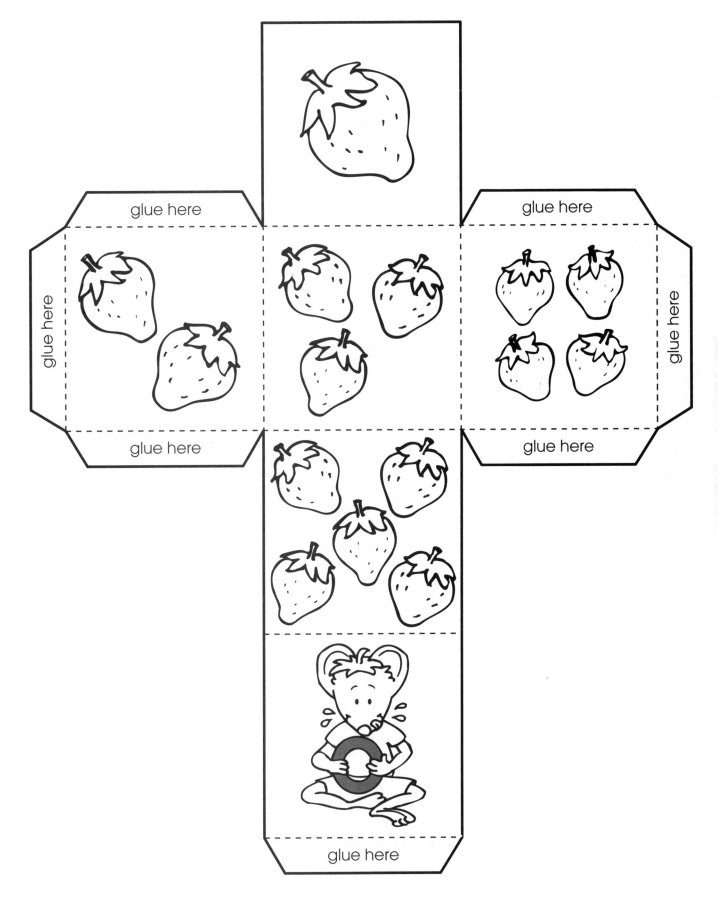

Name _____

To Market, To Market

Cut.
Glue.
Color.

Strawberries 1¢

Each

			1¢	5¢	10¢

Mad About MAGNETS

Use a bit of magnetic force to attract youngsters to these curriculum-related activities.

paper clips
nuts
bolts
metal washers
metal spoon
metal key
nails
wooden block
eraser
crayon
rubber band
rock
coin
plastic counter
screws
craft stick

Packed To Attract

What makes a magnet so attractive? Use this idea to explore the concept of magnetism. To begin, gather a collection of small magnetic and nonmagnetic items (see list) and a shallow box. To create a magnetic board, attach a magnetic sheet to a sturdy piece of cardboard. Share with youngsters that magnets are "packed" with *magnetism,* an invisible force that attracts certain metallic items. Invite each child, in turn, to select an item and predict whether or not it is attracted to magnets. Then have him test his prediction with the magnetic board. If the item is attracted to magnets, it will stick to the board. Instruct students to leave the magnetic items on the board and to put the nonmagnetic items in the box. Afterward, leave the sorted items on display to use as a reference for "Magnetic Memories."

Magnetic Memories

Use the power of magnets to strengthen youngsters' memory skills. To begin, cover the item-filled magnetic board and the box from "Packed To Attract." Then give each child a copy of page 32. Instruct her to place a paper clip on each item that is attracted to a magnet. Have her place a plastic marker on each of the other items. Then uncover the magnetic board and box. Encourage the child to remove each paper clip on her paper with a magnetic wand and then check to see if the item pictured is on the board. Then have her remove each plastic marker and look for that pictured item in the box. Challenge the child to repeat the activity until she correctly marks each magnetic and nonmagnetic item on her page.
Then have her color only the magnetic objects.

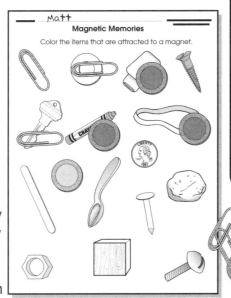

Matt
Magnetic Memories
Color the items that are attracted to a magnet.

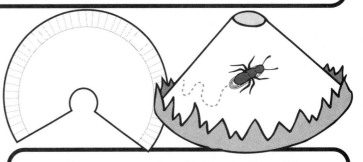

Magnetic "Ant-ics"

This magnetic rhyming activity is sure to attract youngsters' attention. For each child, hot-glue a rubber ant to a paper clip; then cut a large, thin paper plate as shown. To make an ant mound, color the plate brown; then overlap and staple together the edges of the plate. Staple a construction-paper grass strip around the bottom of the mound. Give each child a mound, an ant, and a magnetic wand. Show him how to move the wand inside the mound to make his ant crawl around on the outside. Then have him maneuver his ant to the following rhyme. On the last line, instruct the child to draw the ant into the mound with the wand.

Here's my little ant,
Crawling on his mound,
Crawling up and over
And crawling all around.
He crawls up to the top,
And he crawls right back down.
He crawls and crawls and crawls,
And then he crawls into his mound.

Name_____

Magnetic Memories

Color the items that are attracted to a magnet.

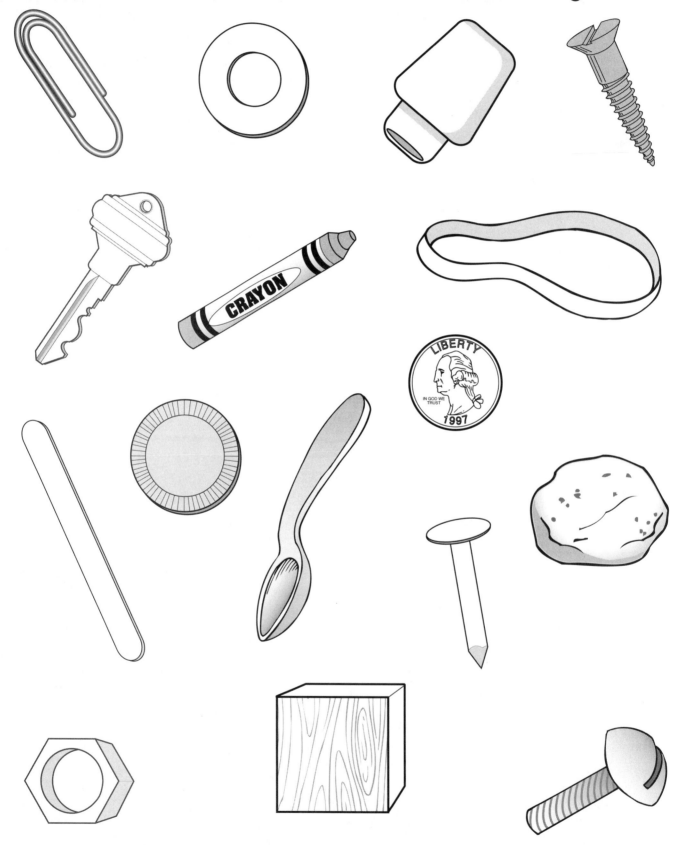

ALL ABUZZ ABOUT BEES

These "un-bee-lievably" fun activities will have your classroom buzzing with busy little learners.

BEES AND ME

Introduce a bit of "bee-ology" and "me-ology" with these student-made comparison books. To prepare, enlarge the beehive on page 38; then duplicate a tagboard beehive and a set of pages 35–37 for each child. Have each child cut out the beehive (to serve as the booklet backing), the booklet pages, and the accompanying pieces. Then assist him in completing the following steps for each set of pages.

BEES

Cover: Color the bees.

Page 1: Color the bee and beehive. Make some thumbprint bees around the hive.

Page 2: Draw a flower on the stem; then color the picture.

Page 3: Glue the stop sign onto the outline. Color the picture.

Page 4: Color the honey jar; then glue it onto the outline. Color the picture.

ME

Draw a picture of yourself and write your name.

Draw your home. Fill in the blank.

Draw something that you like to smell.

Draw a red item; then fill in the blank.

Draw something you can make. Fill in the blank.

After all the pages are completed, sequence each set. Staple the "Bees" pages to the bottom left of the beehive and the "Me" pages to the bottom right. Color the bee cutout; then glue it to the beehive. Invite each child to read his booklet to a partner, then take it home to share with his family.

HONEYCOMB MATH

Sweeten youngsters' math skills with this honey of an idea. Program a copy of page 38 with simple addition or subtraction problems; then duplicate a copy for each

student. Give each child a cup of Honeycomb® cereal to use as manipulatives. Have him solve the problems and then write his answers on his paper. Then ask each child to exchange his paper with a classmate to have his answers checked for accuracy. After completing the exercise, invite youngsters to take the sting out of their appetites with a Honeycomb® snack.

"ALPHA-BEES"

Here's a "bee-ginning" sounds activity that's sure to fly with your students! Duplicate a supply of the bee pattern on page 37. Cut out each pattern; then program each with a letter. During group time, ask each child to tape a bee cutout to an item beginning with the corresponding letter sound. Review each child's choice and the letter sound. Then give each child a copy of page 39 to complete for independent practice.

1, 2, 3, AS BUSY AS A BEE

Your little honeys will be all abuzz about this numeral writing and sequencing activity. Duplicate a class quantity of page 40. Provide each child with her copy and a set of 25 bean counters. To use, call out a number from 1 to 25 that's written on the sheet; then instruct each child to count out that number of beans. Have the child check her counting by placing one bean in each beehive section up to that number. Continue in this fashion, calling out numbers in random order, until student interest wanes. Then ask each child to write the missing numerals to complete the counting sequence on her beehive.

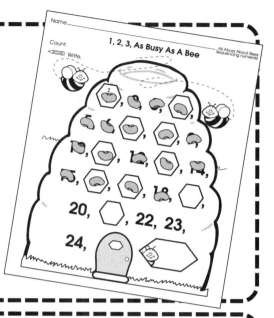

HONEY OF A HOME

Improve your little ones' estimating and counting skills with this honey-of-a-home beehive activity. Duplicate a class supply of a reduced copy of the beehive on page 38. Explain that each child will create a swarm of thumbprint bees to live in his beehive. Then ask each student to estimate the number of bees he thinks will fit in his beehive. Record his guess on the back of his beehive; then invite him to fill his beehive with thumbprint bees, drawing the wings and other bee features on each bee with a marker. After his beehive is full, have the child count the actual number of bees in it. Then write that numeral on the back of the hive with a different color of marker from the written estimate. Have the child compare the two numbers. How close was his estimation to the actual number? To extend this activity, ask each child to circle the bees in groups of ten, then report his results to the class.

BEANIE BEES

Youngsters will make a beeline to the art center to make these "bee-utiful" pictures. In advance, spray-paint a supply of lima beans yellow. Duplicate and cut out several tagboard beehives (page 38) to use as tracers. Put the beans and tracers in the art center.

To make a picture each child traces, cuts out, and glues a construction-paper beehive onto a large sheet of construction paper. She draws an outdoor scene—with trees, flowers, and grass—around the beehive. Then she uses a marker to draw bee stripes and facial features on a few beans. She glues the beanie bees onto the scene, then draws additional bee features for each bee, such as wings, antennae, and a stinger.

After the glue dries, send each of your busy little bees to the writing center to label paper strips with words for the different items in her picture. Or write her dictated story about her bee scene on a separate sheet of paper. Attach each child's word strips or story to her picture; then display all the pictures with the title "Busy Beanie Bees."

Bees

And Me

by _____

©1998 The Education Center, Inc.

Bees live in a hive.

I live in a

_____.

1

1

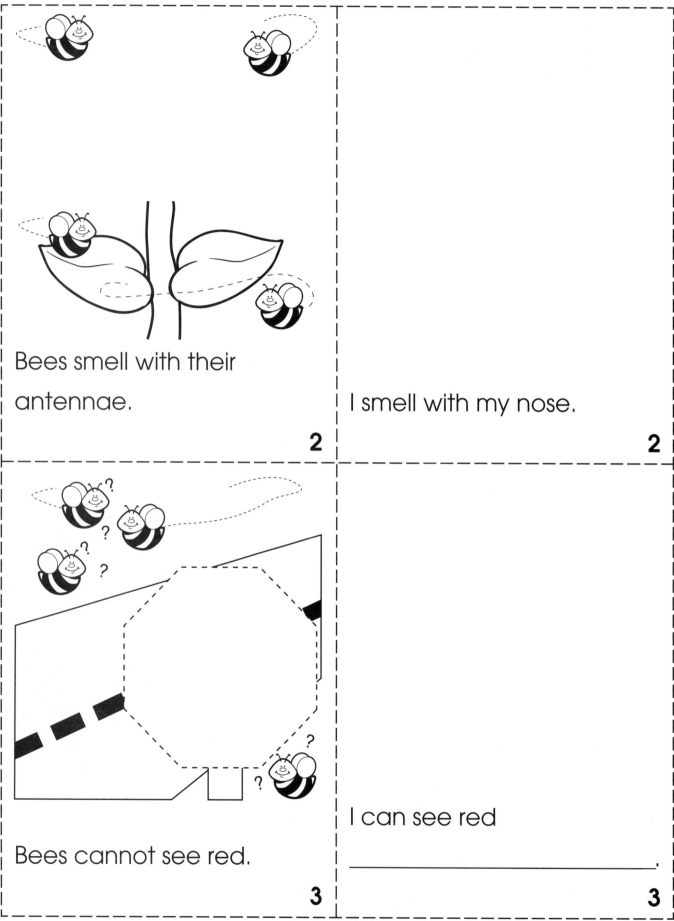

Bees smell with their antennae.

2

I smell with my nose.

2

Bees cannot see red.

3

I can see red

_____.

3

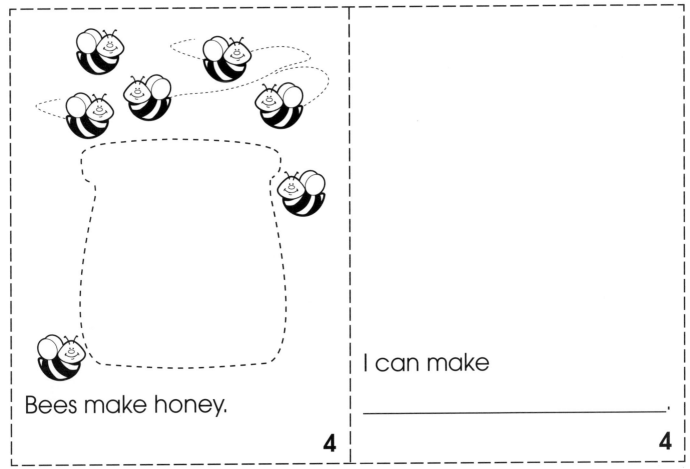

Bees make honey.

4

I can make

_____

4

Booklet Pattern Pieces

Use with "Bees And Me" on page 33. Use the bee pattern with " 'Alpha-Bees' " on page 33.

Honey

STOP

Beehive

Use with "Bees And Me" and "Honeycomb Math" on page 33
and "Honey Of A Home" and "Beanie Bees" on page 34.

©1998 The Education Center, Inc. • *May Monthly Reproducibles* • Kindergarten • TEC951

"Alpha-Bees"

Color the pictures that match the beginning sounds.

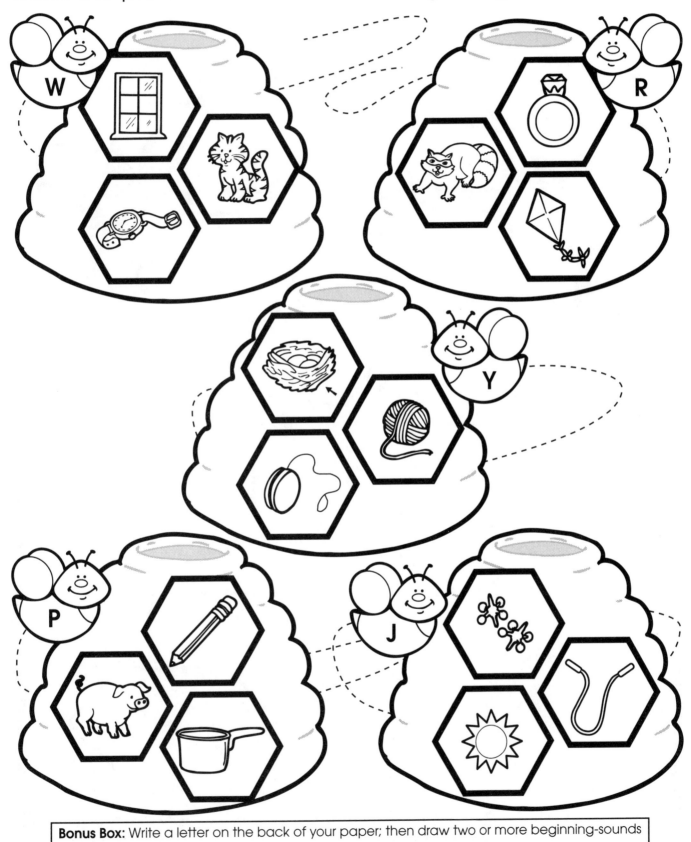

Bonus Box: Write a letter on the back of your paper; then draw two or more beginning-sounds pictures for the letter.

1, 2, 3, As Busy As A Bee

Count.

Write.

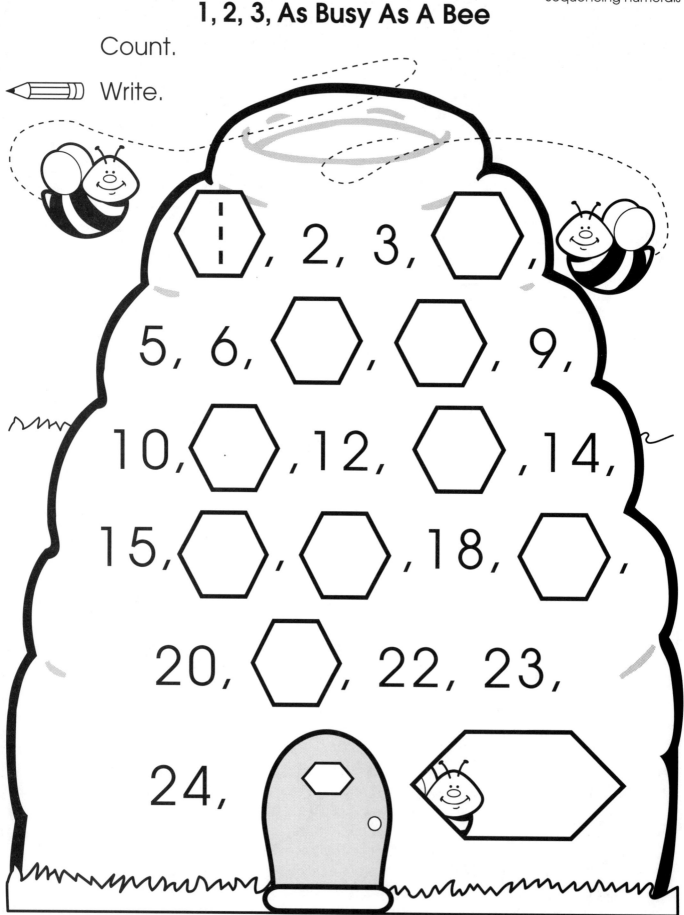

1, 2, 3, ,

5, 6, , , 9,

10, , 12, , 14,

15, , , 18, ,

20, , 22, 23,

24,

It's Picnic Time!

These playful picnic ideas are perfect for leading youngsters into preparations for the real thing. Let's go picnicking!

Picnic Memories

Here's a Memory game to help your class anticipate a picnic-to-be. To prepare, make two copies of the game cards on page 42. Cut out and color each card; then glue each one onto a small paper plate. To play, invert each plate on a table so that the pictures are facedown. Invite a player to turn over two plates to look for a match. If he finds a match, he keeps the plates. Otherwise he returns the plates facedown. Have players take turns in this fashion until all the matches are found. Then ask each player to tell how the pictures on his card pairs relate to a picnic. Sweet memories!

5 apples

4 bananas

Go Picnicking!

Youngsters will get hooked on this picnic-style version of Go Fish. To make the cards, duplicate two construction-paper sets of the game cards on page 42. Color and cut out the cards; then glue each to the face of a separate card from an old playing-card set. If desired, laminate the cards for durability. To play, deal five cards to each of two players. Place the remaining cards in a facedown stack on the table; then instruct youngsters to play the game like Go Fish, with one exception—the words "Go Fish" are replaced with "Go Picnicking." After all the matches are made, invite youngsters to shuffle the cards for another round of play…and another…and another!

A Perfect Picnic

Your little picnickers will pack their imaginations with picnic preferences when they create this class booklet. Duplicate and cut out two construction-paper copies of the booklet cover on page 43 and a class quantity of a booklet page on page 44. Ask each child to illustrate his booklet page with an item he would like to pack for a perfect picnic; then have him write/dictate a completion to the sentence. Put the booklet covers back-to-back; then stack and staple the students' pages between them. Title the front cover "Our Perfect Picnic." Share the booklet with your class, inviting each child to read his page. Then refer to the booklet for items to pack when you plan your *real* picnic. What a picnic-perfect idea!

Our Perfect Picnic

Stacy will bring

cupcakes for our picnic.

Game Cards

Use with "Picnic Memories" and "Go Picnicking!" on page 41.

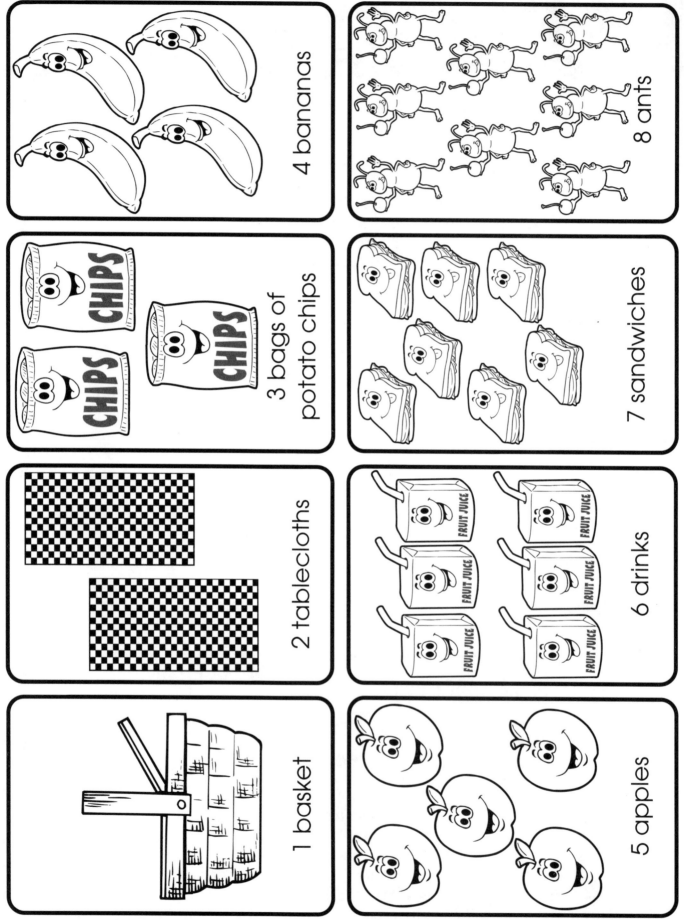

4 bananas

8 ants

3 bags of potato chips

7 sandwiches

2 tablecloths

6 drinks

1 basket

5 apples

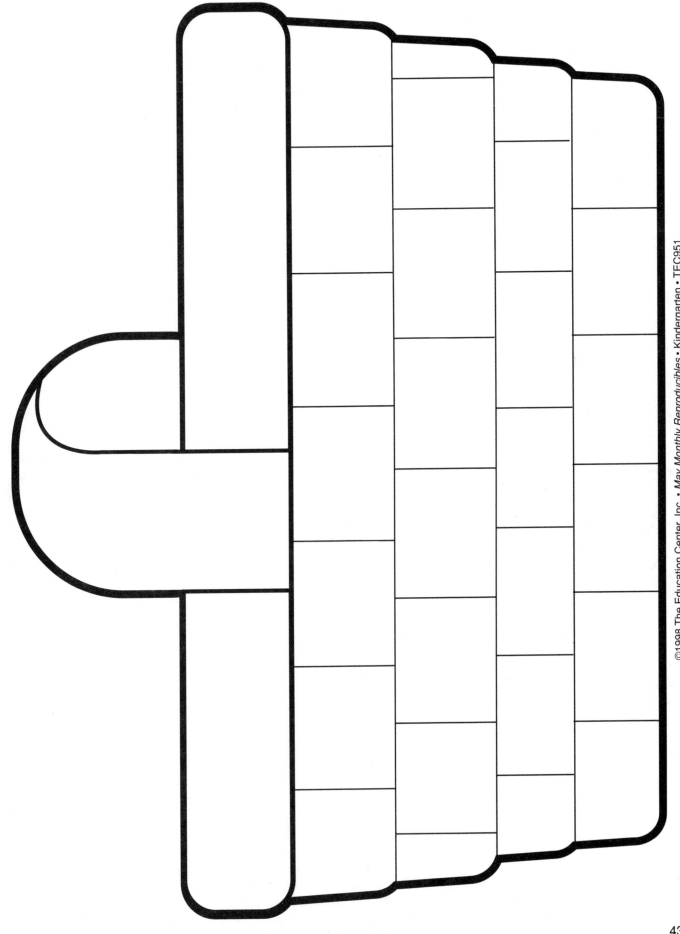

Booklet Pages

Use with "A Perfect Picnic" on page 41.

_____ will bring

_____ for our picnic.

_____ will bring

_____ for our picnic.

Flights Of Fancy

Invite your little nature lovers to flutter into the fanciful world of butterflies with this collection of fun and creative activities.

Emerging Butterflies

A caterpillar gets so wrapped up in cocoon building that, in no time, it discovers that it has turned into a butterfly! When youngsters make these emerging butterflies, they'll also get wrapped up in that wonderful transformation—and the beautiful butterfly surprise. Duplicate a class supply of page 46. Have each child color heavily along the outline of her butterfly with a crayon. Then have her erase back and forth over the colored outline to create a feathered effect. (If she desires, allow her to add more erasure designs to her butterfly.) Instruct the child to cut out her butterfly and poem. To make a cocoon, glue the poem on a cardboard tube as shown. To make a butterfly, glue two wiggle eyes onto the butterfly cutout; then glue the cutout onto a wide craft stick. After the glue dries, carefully roll the butterfly wings towards its middle. Slide the butterfly into the cocoon. Teach youngsters the poem, singing it to the tune of "The Itsy Bitsy Spider." At the appropriate time, signal children to release their butterflies from the cocoons. Beautiful!

Butterfly Garden

Celebrate the arrival of spring, Mother's Day, or just the beauty of butterflies with this special garden. To prepare, duplicate a class quantity of the flower and leaf patterns on page 50 onto construction paper. Laminate and cut out the patterns; then cut out the hole as indicated on each flower. Place the patterns in a center along with a supply of six-ounce Styrofoam® cups, pastel cupcake liners, regular and gold-tinsel pipe cleaners, glue, and green crinkled-paper strips.

To make a butterfly, flatten and gather a cupcake liner to form wings; then twist a pipe cleaner around the liner, inserting a short length of gold pipe cleaner to serve as the antennae. Glue a leaf cutout onto a flower cutout; then slide the flower onto a cup until it fits snugly around the rim. Fill the cup with crinkled-paper strips. Bend or cut the pipe-cleaner stem on each butterfly to the desired length; then insert each stem into the cup. Display the gardens in a prominent place. Or invite each youngster to take hers home to give to a special person. Everyone will be all aflutter over these gardens!

Butterflies...A To Z

Take an up close and personal look at butterfly wings—and the alphabet—with *The Butterfly Alphabet* by Kjell B. Sandved (Scholastic Inc.). After sharing the book with your class, put it in a center with a magnifying glass to entice youngsters to take a closer look. As a follow-up, give each child a copy of pages 47–49. Have her complete each page according to the following directions:

Page 47: Examine the pattern on each butterfly's left wing; then reproduce the pattern on the right wing.

Page 48: Write the letter to complete each sequence on the page.

Page 49: Color all the dotted sections on a butterfly the same color to reveal the letters. Color the remaining sections of each butterfly's wings a different color.

Butterfly And Poem Patterns

Use with "Emerging Butterflies" on page 45.

The little caterpillar
Will spin its own cocoon.
There it will rest for
Changes to come soon.

Out comes an insect
With brand-new wings to try.
Now the little caterpillar
Is a butterfly!

Name _____

Copycat Butterflies

Look.

 Draw matching wing patterns.

 Color.

Butterflies...A To Z

Write the missing letters.

N __ P   X Y __   __ __ D E

__ N O   __ B C   T __ V

U V __   K __ M   __ G H

__ C D   Q __ S   I J __

Winged Surprises

Color the letter hidden in each wing.

Bonus Box: Draw a butterfly on the back of your paper. Hide a letter in its wings.

Cut this out.

Nature's Irresistible Charms: Rocks, Dirt, & Mud

Kids just can't resist rocks, dirt, and mud! So invite your young naturalists to dig into these curriculum-related nature activities. They'll be charmed!

Rock Roundup

Here's a really rocking idea to rouse your youngsters' curiosity about rocks. To prepare, equip each child with a plastic-spoon shovel and a large, zippered plastic bag. Wheel a wagon outdoors with the class to take a nature hike. Invite students to assume the roles of roving rock hounds searching for those special finds. Encourage them to round up a collection of interesting rock colors and shapes. Haul their larger finds in the wagon. Back in the classroom, have youngsters display their rock discoveries with the title "Rock Roundup." Then give each child a copy of pages 52 and 53 to complete independently.

"Mud-nificent" Masterpieces

Can you paint with mud? Let your youngsters answer this question with these messy, muddy masterpieces. Supply your art center with a pail of mud, paint containers, an assortment of paintbrushes, water, and a variety of painting surfaces—such as paper, cardboard, wood, textured wallpaper, and bubble wrap. Invite youngsters to don a smock, then set to work mud-painting on selected surfaces. Encourage them to mix different combinations of mud and water in separate containers to find the best paint consistency for each surface. After the masterpieces dry, ask youngsters to select some mud-paintings to display in the nature center. "Mud-nificent!"

Rock Around The Clock

Invite your class to keep on rocking—around the clock, that is—with this time-telling activity. For each child, duplicate the clock and hand patterns on page 54 onto tagboard. Have the child cut out the clock hands; then help him attach the hands to the clock face with a paper fastener. Instruct him to count out a quantity of small stones (or aquarium gravel pieces) corresponding to each numeral on the clock. Then have him glue each stone set onto the appropriate circle. To use, write a time on the chalkboard to indicate a time for a class activity. Ask each student to set his clock to that time. After several rounds of class clock setting, invite youngsters to practice setting their clocks to the times labeled on their papers. Send youngsters and their time-pieces home to rock around the clock with family members.

Name Jonathan
Rocks, Dirt and Mud
Telling time
Rock Around The Clock
Set the clock for each time.

Name _____

52

Rock Roundup

✂ Cut out.   Sequence.   ⌂ Glue.

1	2	3	4

A Double Take

Count each child's rocks.

Graph the amounts.

Color the picture.

Bonus Box: Who has the *most* rocks?

Name _____

Rock Around The Clock

Set the clock for each time.

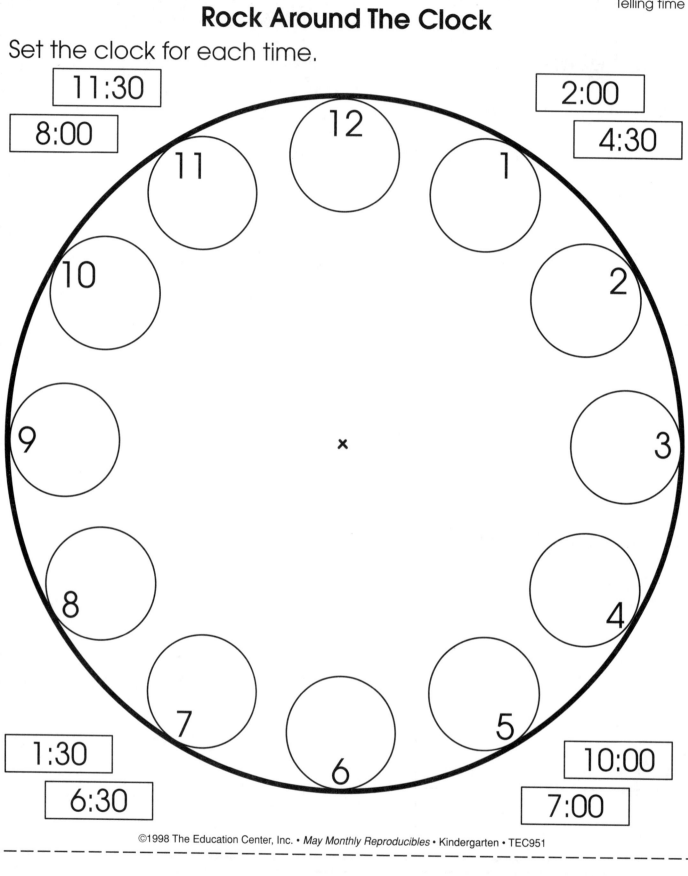

11:30

8:00

2:00

4:30

1:30

6:30

10:00

7:00

54

GOIN' ON A SAFARI

Suit up, grab your binoculars, and head for the grasslands. Your little explorers will be wild about this adventurous skills safari!

Safari 'Round The School

Youngsters will be full of wonder when they go on this spectacular school safari. In advance, duplicate a class quantity of page 58 and varying amounts up to ten of each animal picture on pages 56 and 57 (enlarge the pictures, if you choose); then color and cut out the pictures. Randomly display them on walls, windows, doors, and other school areas. Record the number of each animal displayed. Then equip each child with a copy of the graph, a clipboard, and a crayon. Explain that your class will go on a safari around the school. Each time a child spots one of the animals on his graph, he will color in a box above that animal. After your safari, have youngsters share their results with the class. Did they find all the animals? Which did they spot the most/least?

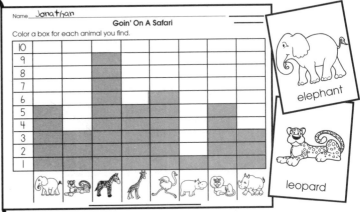

- I can use my trunk like a hand, but I can also breathe and smell with it. *(elephant)*
- I have tan fur and black spots. I like to climb trees. *(leopard)*
- I spend my days resting, eating, and swimming. *(hippopotamus)*
- I can eat leaves from high branches because I am the tallest of all animals. *(giraffe)*
- Even with my large wings, I can't fly. But I can run very fast. *(ostrich)*
- The color of my fur and mane help me to hide in the grasslands. *(lion)*
- I have a unique striped pattern on my horselike body. *(zebra)*
- One or two horns grow from my nose, while three toes grow on each of my feet. *(rhinoceros)*

Have You "Herd"?

Use this herd of safari animals to challenge your students' listening skills. For each child, duplicate a set of the animal pictures on pages 56 and 57. Have each child cut out her pictures, then spread them out in front of her. Explain that after you read an animal fact (see provided facts), each child will decide which animal was described and then hold up that picture. After several rounds, invite youngsters to color their pictures; then have them take the pictures home and share some animal facts with their families. To extend this activity, bring in books about the different animals. Invite youngsters to safari through the books to discover new animal facts.

Take a bite out of basic skills with more safari-themed reproducibles on pages 59 and 60.

Animal Pictures

Use with "Safari 'Round The School" and "Have You 'Herd'?" on page 55.

elephant

leopard

giraffe

zebra

Use with "Safari 'Round The School" and "Have You 'Herd'?" on page 55.

ostrich

hippopotamus

rhinoceros

lion

Goin' On A Safari

Color a box for each animal you find.

10										
9										
8										
7										
6										
5										
4										
3										
2										
1										

Name _____

Safari Sounds

Cut.

Match.

Glue.

©1998 The Education Center, Inc. • *May Monthly Reproducibles* • Kindergarten • TEC951

h	l	z
r	e	o

59

Name _____

Animal Addition

Count each animal.
Write the numeral.
Add.

©1998 The Education Center, Inc. • *May Monthly Reproducibles* • Kindergarten • TEC951

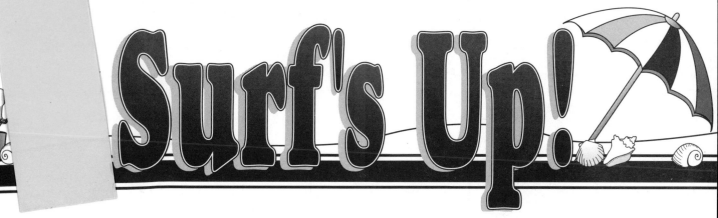

Surf's Up!

Surf into these exciting beach-related activities for a splashing good time.

Have Beach Bag, Will Travel

Load up the beach gear and head for the surf! When youngsters fill this beach bag, they'll be packing some classification skills along with it. In advance, pack a beach bag with an assortment of items—some appropriate for a beach excursion, and some not. Then, for each child, duplicate the beach-bag cards (page 62) on construction paper.

Show youngsters the beach bag; then invite volunteers, in turn, to remove an item from the bag. Discuss whether or not the item is appropriate to take to the beach. Then give each child a white paper lunch bag and a set of cards. Have her decorate her bag with beach-themed stickers, sponge-paintings, or drawings; then help her attach a yarn handle to her beach bag. Instruct the child to color and cut apart her cards. Then have her pack her beach bag with only those cards picturing items appropriate for a trip to the beach. Let's go!

Shells And Cents

Your little beachcombers will be right on the money with this coin-recognition game. To prepare a gameboard, duplicate the game patterns on page 63. Make a few extra copies of the starfish and crab; then copy a larger supply of the scallop and sand dollar. Color and cut out each pattern. Title a piece of poster board "Down By The Sea." Glue the cutouts onto the poster board to form a path, as shown. Paint around the path with water-thinned glue; then sprinkle a layer of sand over the glue. Shake off the excess sand. Then put the gameboard; a supply of small seashells; and a small bag of pennies and nickels in a center.

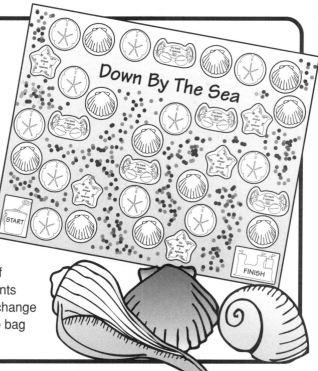

To play the game, explain that each player draws a coin from the bag, then moves his shell game marker the number of spaces represented by the coin. For example, a nickel represents five spaces. After all players reach the finish, invite them to exchange their coins for keepsake seashells. Then return the coins to the bag for the next round of play.

See More At The Seashore

Oh, the sights you'll see when you're down by the sea! And youngsters are bound to count this imaginary beach excursion a colorful trip. To prepare, duplicate page 64 for each child. Have her color each item at the bottom of the page a different color; then have her find the items in the large picture and color them accordingly. Direct her to count each item and write the numeral on the corresponding line. Ahhh, the sea!

Beach-Bag Cards

Use with "Have Beach Bag, Will Travel" on page 61.

flippers	mittens	radio
teakettle	suntan lotion	sand bucket
flip-flops	swim trunks	snorkel
camera	fan	diving mask

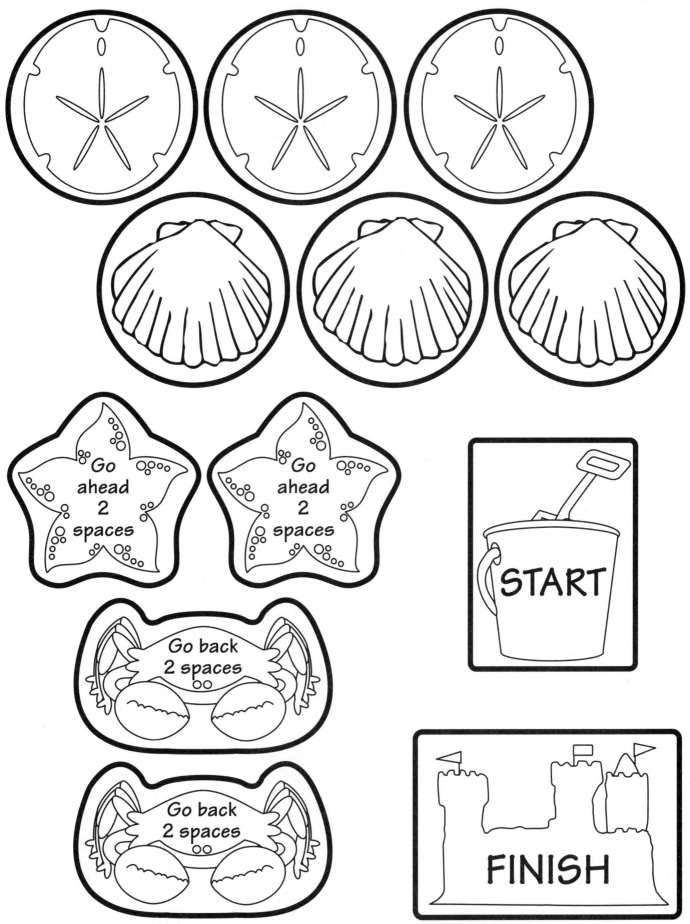

Go
ahead
2
spaces

Go
ahead
2
spaces

START

Go back
2 spaces

Go back
2 spaces

FINISH

Name

Beach Buddies

Color. Count. Write.